# Handy Guide to Self-Publishing

# Handy Guide to Self-Publishing

Founder of P.H. Village Publishers, LLC and
Self-Published Author:

## Teressa I. Leath

P.H. VILLAGE PUBLISHERS, LLC • Pennsylvania

First Printing 2008


Published by P.H. Village Publishers, LLC
P.O. Box 1007
Westtown, PA 19395
www.phvpub.com
610-399-0645

Library of Congress Control Number: 2007906580
ISBN: 978-0-9763131-1-3


Cover Image: IStockphoto.com
Cover Layout: John Morris-Reihl
Graphs Layout: Timothy T. Leath of T. Leath Consulting, LLC

*To my heart's desire*
*my husband, Tim*

*As always, thank you for your constant love*
*and technical support.*

*To my sister Carol Brown*
*and best friend Vernetta Blue*

*I'm truly grateful for your support in*
*helping me bring this together.*

*"May the grace of the Lord Jesus Christ and the love of*
*God and the fellowship of the Holy Spirit be with you."*
*Corinthian: 13:14*

# Table of Contents

# *A Note from the Author*

"How did you get started writing?" and "Who published your book?" are two questions people always ask me when I'm on tour. Once they learn I self-published, they want to know how I did it. They would like to do the same thing but have no clue how to begin the process. Whether it's getting started with writing or self-publishing a book, it's the "getting started" part that is the drawback for most people.

After I finished my first novel, *And Then Some*, I founded P.H. Village Publishers, LLC in January 2005 to publish and promote my work. I knew I wanted it in print immediately. I didn't want to wait several months for a traditional publisher to let me know if they would publish my book. I also didn't want to spend additional time waiting to hear back from a literary agent (some traditional publishers require you to have one) for a decision on whether or not to represent me.

My advice to those who ask how to start writing is always the same and very simple: Just do it! The number one response I get from people is, "I don't have the time." The problem with that is you won't find the time as long as you keep *telling* yourself you don't have time. Skip your nightly phone chat with a friend, pass up watching a TV program, or don't check your e-mail for the third time in the day, and you will be amazed at how much time you'll find. All it takes for you to begin is to write your first sentence, whether it's in Word on your home computer or on a napkin while sitting at a restaurant. You will find that the rest will follow more easily, and you will be amazed at how much you can accomplish once you're determined to do so.

Many have asked, "I want to self-publish, but where do I begin?" You've written your manuscript. Where do you go from there? The *Handy Guide to Self-Publishing* is designed with you in mind.

Whether you've completed your manuscript or are in the middle of it, this booklet will help guide you through the necessary steps to complete your self-publishing mission.

Learning how to self-publish took a lot of time, patience, and dedication on my part. It was an enjoyable experience for which I am truly grateful. In this booklet, I will teach you to do the same thing, true, one-hundred-percent self-publishing. That means you will start your *own* business and run everything from A through Z. How long it takes you to prepare your manuscript to go to print depends on how much time you dedicate to your mission. I spent a total of two years, seven and a half months writing my novel, researching how to self-publish, and getting my manuscript "press ready" for the printer.

It is my hope that through my dedication and hard work, those of you who also aspire to write will learn how you, too, can explore what I call: *"An Author's Pathway from Inspiration to Realization."*

Peace and Blessings

# Introduction

I awoke that particular morning filled with anticipation. It was the day UPS would deliver that special something to my house, that something that meant, "I did it!" I had accomplished something I'd been working on for over two years, and it was no longer a dream. It was a reality. All of my diligence and patience had finally paid off. And I had much to be thankful for and much to feel good about.

I had to go to work that day. I couldn't hang around the house waiting, as much as I wanted to, for that special box. Instead, I prepared myself as I normally would for a full day of work as an accountant. I knew when I returned home, though, that I would graciously wear another hat, that of an author, because now my dream was tangible.

UPS made the delivery around ten o'clock. Fortunately, my husband was working from home that day, and he called me when it arrived. What did I do when I got the news? The only thing I could do. That's right! I left work as fast as I could and drove home bursting with excitement. So what if it was only ten in the morning? I considered it a much-needed early lunch break and off I went. Wait until the end of the day to see my dream become a reality? Impossible. I had to see it. I had to hold it in my hands as soon as I could.

Wow! That's what I said when I arrived home and tore open the first box. My dream of seeing my manuscript as a finished book had come true. I jumped up and down, glowing, with a huge grin on my face. Once again, this is the part I call, "An Author's Pathway from Inspiration to Realization."

Now it's your turn. Get ready to tear open your first box of that special something, and feel the joy of knowing what you have accomplished!

# Section I

# Establishing Your Business

## Self-Publishing "Road Map"

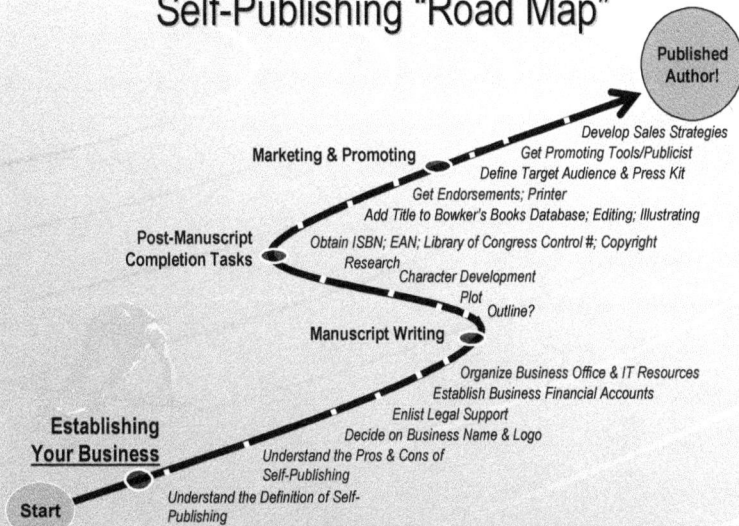

Published Author!

Develop Sales Strategies
Get Promoting Tools/Publicist

**Marketing & Promoting**

Define Target Audience & Press Kit
Get Endorsements; Printer
Add Title to Bowker's Books Database; Editing; Illustrating

**Post-Manuscript Completion Tasks**

Obtain ISBN; EAN; Library of Congress Control #; Copyright
Research
Character Development
Plot
Outline?

**Manuscript Writing**

Organize Business Office & IT Resources
Establish Business Financial Accounts
Enlist Legal Support

**Establishing Your Business**

Decide on Business Name & Logo
Understand the Pros & Cons of Self-Publishing
Understand the Definition of Self-Publishing

**Start**

*"An Author's Pathway from Inspiration to Realization!!"*

# Section I: Establishing Your Business

To run an effective business, you must first understand the type of business you will be operating. There are also several components necessary for running an efficient business. This section will give you a more in-depth understanding of what self-publishing is and will provide several vital factors for operating your business.

## Gain Background Definition of Self-Publishing

Self-publishing is the fastest growing segment in today's book publishing industry. Self-publishing has gained new respect, and authors are turning more and more to self-publishing as an alternative to traditional publishing. Self-publishing, for many, is the answer to a dream come true. To self-publish in the *true* sense of the word means you are the publisher as well as the author. As the publisher, you will pay for the *full cost* of producing your book(s). You will be responsible for, and have control over, the publishing process, production, marketing, and distribution.

## Understand the Pros and Cons of Self-Publishing

The main benefit to self-publishing is that you hold all rights to your title. You also have total control over areas of publishing you wouldn't have with a traditional publisher such as: when your book is released, the look of your book cover, and the title of your book. Basically, you would have complete control over the production. Another great benefit to self-publishing is that all revenue received from book sales is exclusively yours. On the other hand, self-publishing demands a lot of your time. You will, most likely, at least in the beginning, hold every position from mailroom clerk to CEO. And you will be responsible for all operating costs.

### Decide on a Name for Your Business

Choose a name that is catchy and/or meaningful to you. If forming a limited liability company (LLC) or a corporation, keep in mind that the name must comply with the rules of your state's LLC or corporation division. For instance, if forming an LLC, the name must end with an LLC indicator such as LLC, L.L.C, or Ltd.

I created my company name in the eleventh hour of getting my first manuscript into the "press ready" status my printer required. It wasn't until I went to typeset my title page that I realized I didn't have a business name. Panic stricken, I turned to my husband for help. He was a bit sleep-deprived from being up all night assisting me with technical issues, and he was in somewhat of a silly state. First, we weeded out all of the "creatively challenged" names he provided. Finally, we settled on P.H. Village Publishers, LLC. We created my company's name out of the areas where we grew up in our hometown. My husband was raised in an area called "Park Heights," and I grew up in "Edmondson Village," hence the name "P.H. Village Publishers."

### Create a Logo for Your Company

Your logo should represent your company's principles or name. There are software packages that assist you in doing this. If you aren't skilled in this area, don't worry. Outsource to someone who is, and stay focused on your writing.

### Enlist Legal Support for Setting up Your Business

There are three different types of business structures from which you may choose to set up your business: a limited liability company (LLC), a sole proprietorship, and a corporation. An attorney *is not required* to establish an LLC, but is with a sole proprietorship and a corporation. All states allow you to form your own LLC by filing articles of organization, the necessary paperwork to establish your company's existence. I recommend using an attorney, if feasible.

Hire an attorney who can handle all requirements to set up your business. If you don't already have an attorney, get a recommendation from a trusted individual, research via the Internet, or contact a few law firms on your own.

Meet with the attorney before hiring him or her, to gain a full understanding of what the attorney will do for you, and what fees will be involved. Most attorneys will give you a free initial consultation. It is important that you feel totally comfortable with whomever you hire, to ensure a good working relationship. Do not feel compelled to hire the first attorney you meet. Allow yourself time to meet with two or three without feeling rushed.

Do some research via the Internet (IRS.gov, etc.), your local library, or a bookstore prior to meeting with your attorney to ensure you know the type of business you want to establish and what questions to ask. Whether you choose a limited liability company, a sole proprietorship, or a corporation, you will need to understand what each will mean to you when it comes to taxes, personal liability protection, and so forth. Before the meeting is concluded, make sure you fully understand the choices you've made.

There are several documents your attorney will need to complete on your behalf. One will be an application for an Employer Identification Number (EIN) also referred to as a Taxpayer Identification Number (TIN) or Federal Tax ID. The EIN will identify your business account, tax returns, and other pertinent documents. If you establish your business as an LLC or sole proprietorship and you *will not* have any employees, you have the option to use your social security number. Although a separate ID number is not required in this case, I recommend using one. Doing so will eliminate potential risk associated with the disclosure of a personal social security number. It also allows you to keep your personal matters discrete and separate from your business matters.

A good thing about having an attorney is he or she will handle all the necessary legal procedures to establish your business. This will make the process painless for you and allow you to focus your energy on writing. Depending on the time of year, this process can be completed within a matter of weeks. Attorneys' fees vary, but it should not be too costly. It is possible to have an attorney handle what you need for less than a thousand dollars.

## Open a Checking Account

It is important to keep your business and personal transactions separate from each other. This is particularly important at tax time. Once you establish your business, open a free business checking account. Notice I said "free checking." These accounts do exist. Shop around by calling different financial institutions and inquire about their free business checking accounts. Do not pay more than you have to. If you're like most self-published authors, you'll need to watch your cash outflow.

## Set up a Merchant Service Account with a Financial Institution

As a publisher, you may miss out on sales if you do not have the capability to accept credit cards. The use of a credit card machine to process customer transactions will be invaluable for your business as you travel around promoting your book. Again, I stress the importance of shopping around. See what is *feasible* for your business by forecasting what your monthly overall sales and credit card transactions will be, before locking yourself into a contract. You can choose from different types of wireless credit card terminals, each with different monthly fees.

## Purchase a Personal Computer, Printer, and Fax Machine

Simply put, if you don't have a computer (or one that works well), buy one. It will be difficult to operate your business without an efficient computer. Today's industry requires using several different software packages that will not operate on an antiquated computer.

You will need a printer that can produce good-quality printouts of your manuscript, invoices, your company correspondence, and any other business-related documents. Be sure your printer is in good working condition so documents appear crisp, clean, and are not smudged.

A fax machine will be a good investment. Enough said.

### Set up a Business Telephone

Install a separate telephone line in your home office as your business line, if feasible. If you're going to use your personal telephone as your business phone, I recommend you purchase an answering machine with multiple voicemail box capability in order to have a separate voice message for your business.

### Order Business Cards

Invest in *professional business cards*, but make sure you shop around. You can find several companies on the Internet that offer cost-effective business cards. See the resource page at the end of this booklet for some suggestions.

### Invest in a Financial Software Package

Purchase a *software program* for your business financial recordkeeping. A program such as QuickBooks® is an easy-to-learn, user-friendly software package that can meet all of your recordkeeping and financial-reporting needs.

### Rent a Post Office Box

Rent a *post office box* to receive all correspondence relating to your business. This also eliminates using your home address.

### Get a Website Presence and E-mail Access

Nowadays, most all businesses have a Website as a vital means of communication. As an author, you will be asked for your Website often. Be sure you have one.

While developing your Web pages, remember not to give too much personal information on your site. Use your P.O. box instead of your home address, and list an alternative number rather than your home telephone number.

E-mail is another vital means of communication in today's world. Simply put, if you don't already have an e-mail account, get one. You may also acquire a free e-mail account through such resources as yahoo.com and Google's Gmail.

## Enlist an Accountant

Hire an accountant, if you do not currently have one, to handle the financial recordkeeping aspects of your business. If you need assistance in obtaining an accountant, ask for a recommendation from a trusted individual. An accountant will ensure that your business complies with your state and federal laws when it's time to file your taxes.

As a taxpayer, you will need to decide on an accounting method for your business. The most popular methods are the *cash method* and the *accrual method*. With the cash method, you report income in the tax year you receive it, and expenses are accounted for in the tax year you pay them. When you use the accrual method, your income is reported in the tax year you earn it, regardless of when payment is received, and you deduct expenses in the tax year you incur them, regardless of when you pay your invoices.

For example, if Baker & Taylor orders thirty copies of your book in November 2007, you would record the sale of those books in November. Payment on the sale would not be received until February of the following year, because B&T's payment method is net ninety days. For tax purposes, if you use the cash method, you would not report the income from the sale of those books for tax year 2007. It would carry over to the following year when payment is actually received. In the accrual method, you would report the income for the thirty books sold to B&T in 2007, even though you would not receive payment until the following year. The same methodology applies to when you incur your expenses and when you pay them.

Make sure, as you conduct business throughout the year, to keep *all* business-related receipts. This will help you at tax time. Purchase a mileage log book from an office supply store to keep track of your business miles whenever you travel by automobile. Whether you're using your car to take you to your next book signing or delivering books to a nearby bookstore, you will need to keep accurate records.

## Organize Your Home Office

Let's face it, the more organized you are, the more efficient and productive you will be. Assuming you already have a desk and chair or something that will serve as your desk, here are a few other items that can aid you in the process of being organized:

- Filing cabinet
- File folders and labels
- Basic office supplies (pens, paper clips, stapler, ruler)
- Desktop organizer
- Storage boxes for prior years' files
- Appointment book

# Section II

# Manuscript Writing Tips

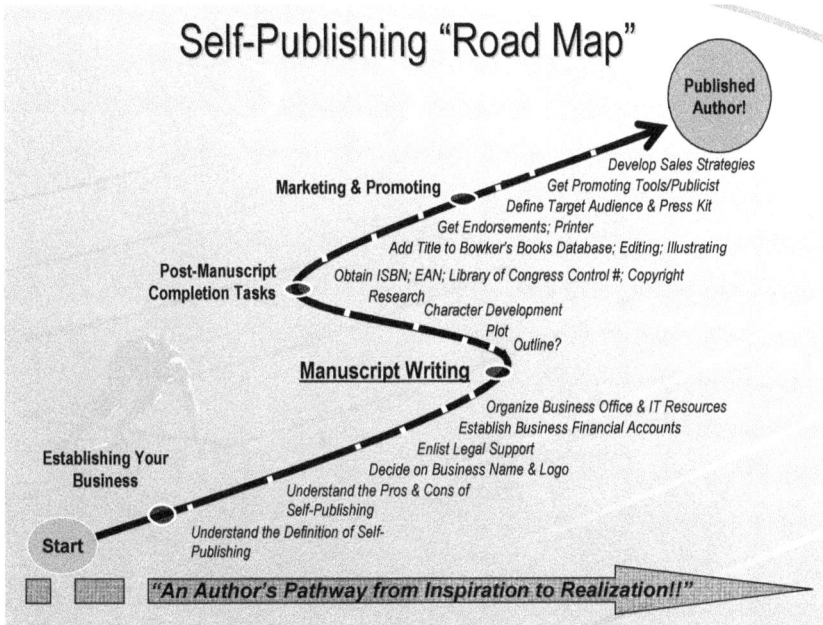

## Self-Publishing "Road Map"

Published Author!

Develop Sales Strategies
Get Promoting Tools/Publicist
**Marketing & Promoting**     Define Target Audience & Press Kit
Get Endorsements; Printer
Add Title to Bowker's Books Database; Editing; Illustrating

**Post-Manuscript**     Obtain ISBN; EAN; Library of Congress Control #; Copyright
**Completion Tasks**     Research
Character Development
Plot
Outline?

### Manuscript Writing

Organize Business Office & IT Resources
Establish Business Financial Accounts
**Establishing Your**     Enlist Legal Support
**Business**     Decide on Business Name & Logo
Understand the Pros & Cons of
Self-Publishing
**Start**     Understand the Definition of Self-
Publishing

*"An Author's Pathway from Inspiration to Realization!!"*

# Section II: Manuscript Writing Tips

Although the *Handy Guide to Self-Publishing* was written as a means to equip you with what it takes to publish a book, I was also inspired to offer a few writing tips. Following are four key tips derived from many conversations I have had with aspiring authors.

### Do You Need an Outline?
Outlining a story is not mandatory before you begin writing. It is an author's choice whether to do so. Some authors choose to jump right into writing and set the flow of the story along the way. Others may need an outline to stay on track with their storyline. Neither is the best way. It is merely an author's preference.

Whichever way you choose, make sure you have an overall concept for the main story of your literary work, the plot, before you begin.

### What Is a Plot?
The plot is your main story. It is a compilation of events that will occur creating the beginning, the middle, and the end of your story. If you need help in structuring a well-written plot, you may want to consider enrolling in a writing course at a local college or university. Seek out writing workshops or writing groups in your area. They may offer help in the various aspects of writing a manuscript.

### Character Development Tip
Understand what types of characters will be in your story and how you plan to use them, and then build their personalities based on that understanding.

For example, if one of your characters is the owner of a small bookstore who is a senior citizen, he or she might be a little *senile*. Use *active verbs* when talking about your character that will draw on the imagination of your readers and help them visualize the scene. For instance, *show* your readers that the store owner is senile through his or her actions rather than *telling* your readers that the character is senile.

An example of "*telling* the reader" the character is senile is: *Mrs. Tart, who is a senile old woman, had trouble waiting on her customer.* An example of "*showing* the reader" that the character is senile is: *Mrs. Tart enters the back of the store for the third time and returns to her customer once again with nothing in her hands, but she carries a well-defined look of perplexity on her face. "What's the name of that book you're looking for?" she asked her customer for the fourth time.*

In the latter example, *showing* your readers the character is senile engages them more in the story.

### Is Research Necessary?
Depending on what you're writing about, you may wish to do some research on your story or a portion of your storyline. Research will add validity to your story. Even if you're writing fiction, readers want to feel a connection to the characters, places, and events within your story. For example, if one of your characters visits a foreign country, though you may never have been there yourself, a little research will allow you to write as if you have been there. The Internet is a wonderful tool for this type of research. Also consider conducting interviews with people who are experts on your particular subject.

# Section III

# You've Written Your Manuscript...Now What?

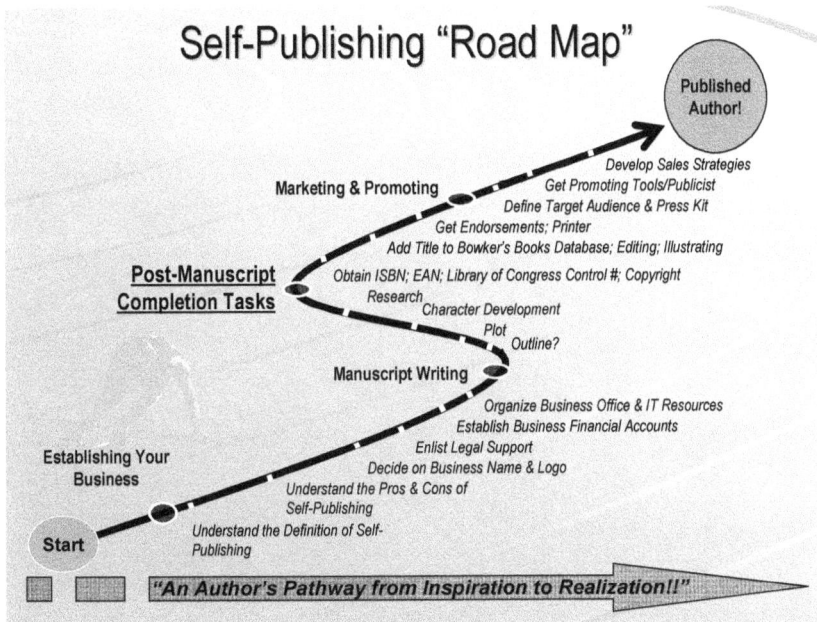

## Self-Publishing "Road Map"

**Published Author!**

Develop Sales Strategies
Get Promoting Tools/Publicist
**Marketing & Promoting**
Define Target Audience & Press Kit
Get Endorsements; Printer
Add Title to Bowker's Books Database; Editing; Illustrating

**Post-Manuscript Completion Tasks**
Obtain ISBN; EAN; Library of Congress Control #; Copyright
Research
Character Development
Plot
Outline?

**Manuscript Writing**

Organize Business Office & IT Resources
Establish Business Financial Accounts
Enlist Legal Support
**Establishing Your Business**
Decide on Business Name & Logo
Understand the Pros & Cons of Self-Publishing
Understand the Definition of Self-Publishing

**Start**

"An Author's Pathway from Inspiration to Realization!!"

# Section III: You've Written Your Manuscript...Now What?

Now that your masterpiece is complete, you will need to do a few things to bring your project to fruition. Following is a list of those items. They are not listed in sequential order, because one doesn't necessarily have to be done before another, and some may be done simultaneously. I will also provide you with insight for a timeline.

- **International Standard Book Number (ISBN):** An ISBN is a 13-digit number used to identify books or book-like products. R.R. Bowker, LLC is the agency that supplies this number. The Website to obtain an ISBN application is www. isbn.org or call (800) 521-8110. Normal turnaround time is about fifteen business days. You will need your ISBN when you submit your manuscript to your printer.

- **Bookland EAN (European Article Number) 13-bar code:** An EAN is to books as a UPC symbol is to most other products sold in the United States. The EAN has a 978 prefix and is used on books internationally. The bar code encodes the ISBN and is used by retailers to scan your product into their readable system when someone makes a purchase. You may obtain the bar code from R.R. Bowker, or check with your printer. Most printers offer this service at no additional charge.

- **Library of Congress Control Number:** The Library of Congress, which is the largest library in the world, will provide the control number for your book. There is not a fee to obtain this number. You will be required, however, to submit to them a copy of your finished book. For general information call (202) 707-5000 or visit their Website at www.loc.gov/index.html. Normal turnaround time to receive your number is about a week.

**Copyright:** Understand that your "work" is considered copyright-protected from the moment it is created in a tangible form. Registering is completely voluntary but is encouraged because of its benefits. If you want the right to initiate a lawsuit for any violation of your work, you will need to register your work with the copyright office. Contact The Library of Congress copyright office at (202) 707-3000 or visit their Website at www.copyright.gov to obtain the proper form to register your literary work. If your submission is in order, you should receive your certificate of registration in about six months. The effective date of registration of your work is the date all required elements in acceptable form are stamped "received" at the copyright office.

- Don't forget to use the copyright symbol © or the word "Copyright" when adding the copyright notice to your title page. Either format is acceptable: © 2007 by John Doe or Copyright 2007 John Doe. Many writers choose to use both.

**Add your title (free of charge) to Bowker's Books In Print database via the BowkerLINK™ system at www. bowkerlink.com:** Books In Print serves as a bibliographic resource to libraries as well as to book trade communities. This tool, which has been in existence for more than fifty years, is used worldwide and provides detailed information about your title and publishing.

**Editor:** Invest in a *professional* editor to edit your manuscript once you have gotten it to a comfortable completion point. You will probably go through several drafts before your manuscript is ready for editing. The editing process can potentially be costly. Editing could run you into the thousands, depending on the size of your manuscript. But this is one place where you do not want to cut corners. You will get what you pay for. I cannot stress this part enough. Do not get caught with countless amounts of errors in your book, as so many self-published authors do. Keep in mind, though, not everyone who claims to be a professional editor is actually an expert. Choose wisely. Before hiring an editor, request a sample edit of a few pages of your manuscript. This will also ensure you choose someone who can edit your work without erasing your voice. It is important to feel comfortable with the editor you hire.

**Cover Illustrator:** The saying, "You can't judge a book by its cover," may be true in the sense that the cover might not be appealing but the story may be good or vice versa. The cover will be the first thing to grab readers' attention and entice them into taking your book from the shelf, especially if you are an as-yet unknown author. You may lose sales based solely on your book cover's lack of appeal. A professional artist or graphic designer can produce an attractive book cover that will stand out from all the rest. Remember to have the title of your book placed on the book cover spine. Although that may sound like simple advice, overlooking a detail such as that could adversely affect the decision of a buyer for a major bookstore.

**Endorsements:** Book endorsements aren't necessary to get a book published. They are a valuable selling tool, and, therefore, worth mentioning. An endorsement from at least one credible source will add to a new author's sales potential. Readers pay attention to what others are saying about a book. Notice I said *credible* source. This does not mean you should not respect your favorite cousin's opinion. Readers, however, are less likely to lend credence to what a relative thinks about your book than they are to a neutral, credible source's endorsement.

Remember to seek out any potential endorsers as soon as your manuscript is in its final stage. You will need to have all endorsements available to your cover illustrator so that he or she can include them on the back cover.

**Printer:** Shop around for a printer that specializes in book binding. Your average corner print and copy place will not fit the bill for the magnitude of this job.

Comparison shop, but don't automatically opt for the cheapest printer. The choice could turn out to be your worst nightmare. Do not assume that your book will turn out as you expect. Ask a prospective printer for samples of their work before making a final decision. Make sure the printer you choose will handle your manuscript in a very professional manner.

In most cases, your book will be bound in what's called "perfect" binding. This is the most popular style and the most preferred binding for bookstores. When selecting and working with a printer, be aware of the following:

- *How long* has the printer been in business and what is the volume of books they produce each year? This will give you an idea for how well their services may be when dealing with your manuscript.

- What is the bottom-line *cost* per unit you will pay for each book? This will play an important role when it comes time to set the *retail* price for your book. A good rule of thumb for setting the retail price is to set it at three and a half times the cost per unit. This will allow you to give wholesaler, distributor, and bookstore discounts and still have a decent profit margin. If three and a half times your unit cost will put your book at a price that *is not* comparable to other books of your kind, then your cost per unit is probably too high. Look into ways to lower your cost such as decreasing the number of pages in your book (this can be done by reformatting your text), ordering a larger quantity of books at one time, or going with another printer altogether to keep your retail price competitive with similar books.

- Inquire about the *printer's turnaround time* for receiving your books. This will allow you to plan such things as your book release party.

- Ask the printer, up front, what *types of files* are acceptable for electronically submitting your text and book cover. Don't wait until you're ready to submit your manuscript, and then discover you don't have the required software to do so.

- Know if the printer requires you to submit your manuscript in a *press ready* status, or if they offer assistance in getting it ready for print. Most printers require that your manuscript be "press ready," meaning no alterations are needed.

As the publisher, you want to produce professional-quality books. The layout you give to your printer is the same layout you will get in return. Most printers do not handle typesetting, and require that your document is "press ready." Don't be in such a rush to have your book printed that you don't take time to examine the proper text layout for a book. The interior of your book should be just as attractive as the exterior. Although you are self-publishing, your book should still have the prestigious appearance of a book produced by a high-end, traditional publishing company.

# Section IV

# Marketing & Promoting

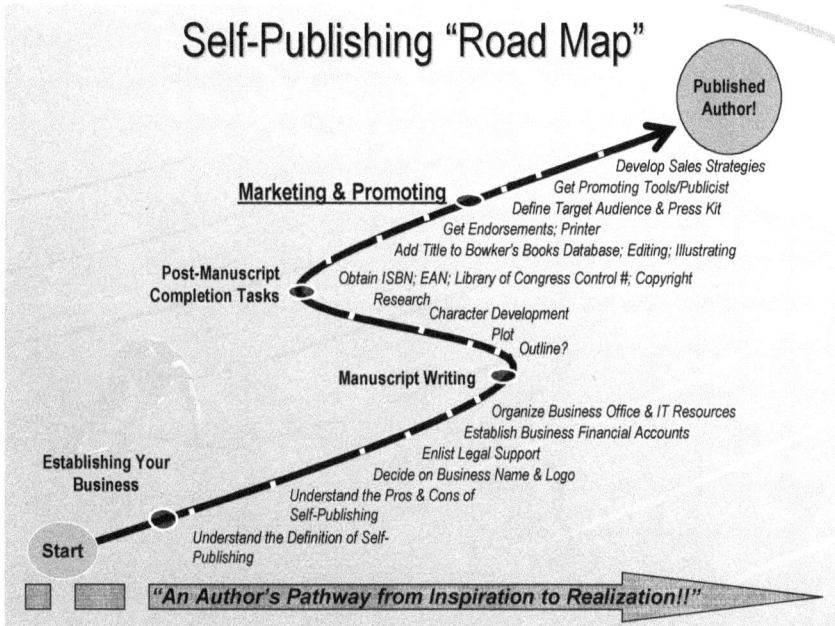

## Self-Publishing "Road Map"

**Published Author!**

Develop Sales Strategies
Get Promoting Tools/Publicist

**Marketing & Promoting**
Define Target Audience & Press Kit
Get Endorsements; Printer
Add Title to Bowker's Books Database; Editing; Illustrating

**Post-Manuscript Completion Tasks**
Obtain ISBN; EAN; Library of Congress Control #; Copyright
Research
Character Development
Plot
Outline?

**Manuscript Writing**

Organize Business Office & IT Resources
Establish Business Financial Accounts
Enlist Legal Support

**Establishing Your Business**
Decide on Business Name & Logo
Understand the Pros & Cons of Self-Publishing

**Start**
Understand the Definition of Self-Publishing

*"An Author's Pathway from Inspiration to Realization!!"*

# Section IV: Marketing and Promoting "Now the Fun Starts"

For many self-published authors, marketing and promoting is the most challenging responsibility because of its time and money demands. Marketing your books will take a lot of dedication on your part. You may experience frustrating times if you are not sure what to do or have help in doing it. In this section, I will discuss some fun and possibly rewarding marketing and promotional strategies.

## What Is Marketing?
To market your book means that you will make your book available for sale through various marketplaces. This may be a bookstore, a book festival, an event that allows vendors, or your own personal Website.

## The Vitality in Promoting
Promoting is a vital part of the life of your book. When you promote, you encourage book sales. The main key to promoting is advertising, whether it's through magazines, online bookstores, your own Website, or other sites. Word of mouth is also a wonderful way to promote your book. Everywhere you go, tell someone about your book. Keep some of your promotional items with you at all times. This way, when the opportunity permits, you can give someone a bookmark or postcard containing information about your book and your Website.

## Who Is Your Target Audience?
Before you can begin marketing your book, you need to ask yourself

one question: Who is my target audience? Your target audience is the group of people most likely to buy your book.

Because you will be investing a lot of your time and resources, it is critical you make wise choices. For example, if you've written a love story, know that your target audience will most likely be women within a certain age group. Chances are you might not sell a lot of copies to men in a barbershop, but the beauty shop just might work. Another example may be for someone who has written a story about the ills of factory farming. This person would want to reach out to all the health conscious and, in particular, animal advocates. A good pitch to the biology department at universities wouldn't hurt either.

**Press Kit ... What Is It?**
A press kit is your resume. It is your sales pitch. This is what you will use to get the attention of prospective book buyers, distributors, and the media. In your kit, include an introduction letter, your biography (one page will do), book reviews, press releases, a sales sheet, marketing and promotional plan, tour schedule of all your upcoming appearances for the current year, promotional items, business cards, suggested interview questions, and a four-by-six-inch, professional-looking photo of yourself.

All of the material in your kit can be placed in a two-pocket, laminated or linen folder with a slit for your business card. The most important pieces in your kit such as your introduction letter, press release, biography, and sales sheet should be placed in the right side of the folder. All other documents may be placed in the left side. Choose a folder color that resembles or coordinates with your book cover color(s). To help your press kit stand out from all the rest, glue or tape a photocopy of your book cover to the front of your folder. Be sure to use high-quality photo paper if you chose to print the cover yourself.

Don't worry if you don't have a lot to place in your kit at first. You will add to it as you go along. Make certain you keep your press kit up-to-date with the latest information about you and your book. And lastly, carry a kit with you wherever you go. You never know when opportunity may strike.

## Promotional Tools

The following list of promotional tools will help you in your marketing process:

- 📖 **Postcards** are a great way to announce the release of your book to friends, family, and others who may be interested in purchasing it. You may also want to give them to retailers to place in customers' bags.

- 📖 **Posters** of your book cover are a great way to attract spectators' attention at any event where you are selling your book.

- 📖 **Bookmarks** are a nice gift for everyone who purchases your book. Be sure to include your Website address on the back of your bookmark.

- 📖 **Calendar magnets** featuring your book will look great on anyone's refrigerator. What better way to give people a gentle reminder than to have them see your book cover every time they check a date or open their refrigerator door?

## Marketing and Promotional Strategies

The following strategies have proven to be very beneficial for marketing the books of new self-published authors. Often, these tactics are overlooked altogether or aren't done in a timely manner. The sooner you take action in making your book available for sale, the greater the benefit. Waiting too long to engage in some of these strategies may affect you adversely.

- 📖 **While your book is at the printer, schedule a release party**

**in your hometown.** Announce your book's release date and the location and time of your party in the local newspaper. If you are able to obtain a radio announcement, that would be a plus. This is clearly something you would need to work on well in advance of receiving the first copies of your book. Timing is crucial.

**Send your book out to several newspapers and magazines to acquire a book review.** A positive book review is a great addition to your press kit. Reviews are also good to have when promoting your book to bookstores and distributors.

**Contact book clubs and introduce your book.** Book clubs are huge and make a significant marketing resource.

**Don't forget about the libraries.** Start by contacting the collection librarians at your local libraries. Send them one of your press kits. Libraries are especially willing to place books on their shelves that a native or former native wrote. Be sure to go back to the town where you were born and raised, if you're no longer a resident, and let the folks back home show their support.

**Tap into the street vendors.** Street vendors are a good resource to load off a box or two of books during the course of a day. New York and D.C. vendors are open to working with self-published authors. If you're willing to walk the pavement and sometimes brave the elements, give them a try.

**Take advantage of book signings in the mall.** While you're working on becoming a well-known author, focus on setting up book signings with bookstores located in the mall, rather than in a strip center. This way you can grab shoppers' attention as they stroll.

📖 **Create your own e-mail/e-blast marketing campaign.** In today's world, just about everyone has an e-mail address. What better way to reach a vast number of people right from your home? Create an e-mail log book, and, when you travel to promote your book, have everyone who expresses an interest sign your log. Even if they purchase your book that day, have them sign. That will give you the opportunity to inform them of future books. The log is also a great way to send a little reminder to those who expressed an interest, but did not make a purchase.

## Good Things to Know Before Vending

As a new self-published author, you will most likely have your eyes and ears fixed on every book-selling opportunity you come across. It is unlikely that you will be able to attend every event, so choose wisely. Choose those events where your selling potential will be the greatest, based on what you're selling and who will be your audience.

Before signing up to become a vendor at any event, ask pertinent questions in addition to the obvious one, How much will it cost to attend? Ask questions such as: How many people are expected at the event? How much time during the event will be allotted for vendors? What type of event is it (if it isn't clear)? Where will the vendor set-up be relative to the main activities? Answers to these questions are just as important as the cost to attend. Remember, the most important key to vending is vendor location.

## What About Book Sales ... How Does That Work?

There are various ways in which you may chose to market your book:

📖 **Independent/direct sales:** This is selling your books without the help of a third party such as a distributor or bookstore. Examples of these types of sales are selling to friends, family, church members, co-workers, and people you do business with (e.g. your dry cleaner, beautician, barber). These are all good resources for your first print run. These types of sales will reap the highest profit margin because you keep one hundred percent of the retail price with little to no cost to you for selling the books.

**Independent/smaller bookstore sales:** For a self-published author, getting into independently owned bookstores will be a lot easier and faster than getting into major bookstores such as Barnes & Noble. Whereas a press kit would be one of the requirements for submission to a major bookstore, for the most part, the owner of an independent store may request only a copy of your book. You can also get started with the smaller stores while you work on preparing your press kit.

The industry standard discount to bookstores is normally around forty percent off the retail price. For example, if your book retails for fifteen dollars, then the store would pay you nine dollars for every copy they sell.

**Wholesalers/distributors:** A wholesaler or distributor is vital for national and international distribution. Major bookstores such as Barnes and Noble and Borders will not order directly from the publisher/author. The wholesaler will offer your book through them for wholesale purchase. A distributor will work at getting your book on bookshelves. The industry standard discount for wholesalers and distributors is between fifty and sixty-five percent off the retail price.

**Sales from book fairs, festivals, conferences, and other events:** To be a vendor/exhibitor can be very beneficial, not only because these types of events normally attract the largest crowds of buyers, but also because this is a great way to network with other authors.

Although you receive one hundred percent of the retail price when selling books at these events, your profit margin will depend on what it cost you to participate as a vendor. Remember when I mentioned how important it is to ask certain questions before deciding if a particular event is right for you? Don't forget those questions. Vendor/exhibitor fees can vary from as little as fifty dollars to as much as three thousand dollars. Weigh your cost against your sales potential, and determine if your product is conducive to potential buyers at a particular event.

## How to Get Your Book in Stores and Online

All authors would love to see their books stocked on bookshelves throughout the county. In today's market, though, brick-and-mortar bookstores aren't the only way to sell a book. Online sales are just as strong and steadily increasing as more and more people are buying over the Internet. As a self-published author, you must work hard to earn buyer recognition for your book, but it can be done. A lot of effort goes into making it a reality, but stay focused on your mission. The following steps will help you do that.

Contact as many *independently owned bookstores* in your area as you can. Tell them you are a local author seeking an opportunity to have your book sold at their store, and inquire about their procedure for doing so. You may find that getting into some independent bookstores will be uncomplicated. Many won't require a press kit, just a copy of your book for them to review.

Find a good *distributor* whose job is to get your book into bookstores. Your chances of national distribution will increase with a distributor working on your behalf. Contact a few distributors and inquire about their submission policy, and then submit to as many as you can. You can never have too many distributors representing your book. At this point, you will need to have completed your press kit, because most distributors will require one.

📖 Contact *Baker & Taylor*, the most widely used wholesaler in the book industry, and sign up to become a vendor. Many online retailers will become aware of your title through Baker & Taylor's database. It's also a good chance that online retailers such as Amazon.com, Wal-Mart, and Borders will pick up your title and make your book available for purchase through them. Keep in mind, although it will be your choice as to the discount you give, when you become a vendor with Baker & Taylor you will increase your chances of more retailers picking up your book if you give the industry standard fifty-five percent. Baker & Taylor will also make other benefits available to you when you give the industry standard.

📖 As previously mentioned, make sure you add your title to **Bowker's Books In Print** database. The database offers complete, unbiased bibliographic information on millions of titles. This is a great resource to booksellers, publishers, and librarians.

Primarily, you want to sell, sell, and sell as many ways as you can. A book that is in high demand is the key to getting book buyers to notice you. Everywhere you go, inform people about your book, and keep spreading the word. When readers start to pour into stores asking if they can get a copy of your book, the bookstores will come looking for you. People must know your book exists for this to happen. Your job, then, is to tell everyone you know, and then have them tell everyone they know.

**Do I Need to Hire a Public Relations Firm/Publicist?**
The job of a publicist is to let the public know your book is available. And an excellent publicist can be vital to your book's success. A lot of energy goes into public relations work. For the majority of self-published authors who are not working as full-time authors, having a publicist is essential. Public relations work can be expensive. Do not jump blindly into using a publicist. Be aware that not everyone who claims to be a publicist will turn out to be a valuable resource. Make sure to research thoroughly any prospective publicist or public relations firm before locking yourself into a contract. Know what your money will or will not get you. You can spend a lot on public relations work, and you will want to spend wisely.

One thing a publicist can do on your behalf is to get you TV and radio interviews. In the beginning, radio interviews will be a lot easier to attain than TV exposure. While you wait, take advantage of talk radio as much as possible. Millions of people listen to the radio on a daily basis, so what better way to reach a large audience? This also includes Internet radio. The key is to increase demand for your book. That will get the attention of book buyers fast. Your publicist should also work to get you book reviews from various newspapers and magazines. Another benefit to hiring a good publicist is he or she can gain national market exposure for you by getting a major distributor to pick up your book. And a distributor's job is to get your book into bookstores.

**Be Your Own Publicist**
Hiring a publicist may not be feasible right away. Don't worry. You can be your own publicist. Who's better at talking about your book than you, the person who knows the most about it? Put as much time into making people aware of your book as you can. After all, that's the job of a publicist, to make the public aware. Contact radio stations, magazines, cable TV stations, book clubs, and schools and universities and solicit your book. Even if

you don't get a positive response immediately, keep at it and stay encouraged.

# *Path Foreword*

Now that you've finished reading this *Handy Guide to Self-Publishing*, you are well on your way to joining many other authors in the book industry. Keep in mind it's important to stay abreast of what's going on in the publishing world and what opportunities are available for self-published authors. Regularly explore the Internet, read publications such as *Publishers Weekly* (available online), *Writer's Market*, and *Writer's Digest*, and be sure to network with other authors as you continue to market your book.

Because you understand the components necessary to publish your book, now would also be a good time to establish an expense budget plan for executing those components. To do this, you can reference the four sections in this book and establish a budget line item for all applicable components.

Remember to stay focused on whatever it is you intend to accomplish throughout your journey. Believe that you can do it, and it will be done.

**My Best Wishes As You Go Forward!**

# *Resources*

**Editing Services:**
Linda Hines – editorlh@bellsouth.net or editorialss@gmail.com
www.book-editing.com
www.pentouch.com
www.writethevision.biz
www.theredpeneditor.com

**Printers:**
Morris Publishing (NE) – www.morrispublishing.com
(800) 650-7888
Lightning Source (TN) – www.lightningsource.com
(615) 213-5815
Thomson Shore Book Manufacturers (MI) www.thomsonshore.com
(734) 426-3939

**Distributors & Wholesalers:**
Midpoint Trade Books (NY) – www.midpointtrade.com
(212) 727-0190
C&B Books Distribution (NY) – www.cbbooksdistribution.com
(717) 591-4525
Afrikan World Books (MD) – www.afrikanworldbooks.com
(410) 383-2006
Independent Publishers Group (IL) – www.ipgbook.com
(312) 337-0747
Seaburn Publishing Group (NY) – www.seaburn.com
(718) 267-7929
Baker & Taylor Books (NC-head quarters) – www.btol.com
(800) 775-1800 or (908) 541-7425

**Advertising & Marketing:**
www.blackbookpromo.com or (630) 524-4579

www.howtomarketmybook.com or (303) 279-4349
www.blackbookplus.com or (877) 227-6977
www.constantcontact.com or (866) 876-8464

## Promotional Items:
www.clubflyers.com or (800) 433-9298
www.printingforless.com or (800) 930-6040
www.edc-creations.com or (301) 434-9446
www.tdmembroidery.com or (610) 431-1919

## Book Cover Design/Layout:
www.dclai.com or art@dclai.com
www.artntech.com or (303) 394-4969
www.kreativewisdom.com or (410) 335-1438
www.mobevisual.com or (410) 262-5459

## Interior Design:
www.pittershawn.com
LindaK Productions – bobkirch_51@msn.com
aMuse Productions – productionwoman@yahoo.com

The information provided here is merely for informational purposes. P.H. Village Publishers, LLC does not endorse the use of any particular company. Use of any resource listed is solely up to the individual's discretion.

# *Glossary*

## *Section I*

**Articles of Organization** – Establishes the existence of your LLC in your state and provides certain basic information about the business.

**Corporation** – A legal business entity having its own rights, power and liabilities separate from its members. A corporation may issue stock either private or public.

**Limited Liability Company (LLC)** – a legal business entity similar to that of a corporation where the owners have limited personal liability for debts and actions. The LLC is not a separate taxable entity.

**Press Ready** – Means that your manuscript is in final layout and ready to print. It will print exactly as it appears. No typesetting or changes are needed.

**Sole Proprietorship** – a business entity owned and operated by one person. The owner of a sole proprietorship and its business is legally inseparable. One and the same.

## *Section III*

**Cost Per Unit** – the price that you will pay per book.

**Distributor** – a company working on behalf of the author or publisher to distribute books to retailers.

**Endorsement** – to gain approval or support for a book.

**Retail Price** – the selling price of a book.

**Perfect Binding** – book pages and cover are held together by a flexible adhesive which is strong and made for long shelf life.

**Profit Margin** – selling price minus the cost per unit.

**Wholesaler** – makes books available for wholesale purchase.

## *Section IV*

**eBlast** – A way to do organize and personalize group emailing without spamming. By using templates it provides for a more professional look.

**Marketing and Promotional Plan** – method used to bring about awareness to the public, thus creating demand for your book

**Press Release** – news article announcing the release of your book and/or upcoming event.

**Sales Sheet** – gives a synopsis and the specification of the book

# Author's Contact Information

Website: www.phvpub.com

Telephone: (610) 399-0645
Address: P.H. Village Publishers, LLC
P.O. Box 1007
Westtown, PA 19395

## Other publications by the author:

And Then Some – a novel

ISBN: 978-0-9763131-0-6